陝西歷史博物館在西安市區的位置圖
The location of the Shaanxi History Museum in Xi'an

咸陽機場
Xianyang Airport

14路巴士路線
No. 14 Bus Routes

飛機場路線
Airport Routes

5路巴士路線
No. 5 Bus Routes

城墙
Wall

館情簡介　藏品精選
Brief Introduction　Selected Treasures

Shaanxi History Museum

陝西歷史博物館

主編尹盛平　副主編李西興
Editor Yin Shengping　Associate Editor Li Xixing

《陝西歷史博物館》編寫組　編
Compiled by Editorial Committee of Shaanxi History Museum
陝西人民美術出版社
香港文化教育出版社　出版
Published by　Shaanxi People's Art Publishing House and
Educational and Cultural Press Ltd. H.K.

館情簡介

陝西歷史博物館館區環境平面圖
The Layout of the Shaanxi History Museum

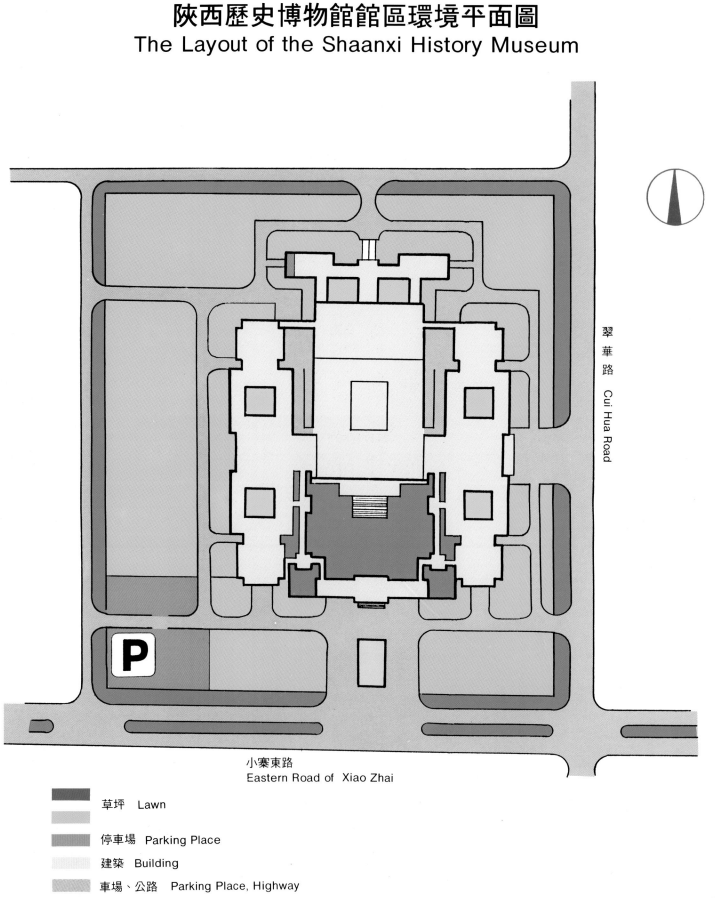

翠華路　Cui Hua Road

小寨東路
Eastern Road of Xiao Zhai

草坪　Lawn

停車場　Parking Place

建築　Building

車場、公路　Parking Place, Highway

天井　Courtyard

水池　Pool

館情簡介
Brief Introduction

概　　況
沿　　革
建築設備
陳列展覽

Survey
Development
Structure & Equipments
Exhibition Halls

陝西歷史博物館全景鳥瞰
A Full View of Shaanxi History Museum

概況
Survey

○ "古都明珠,華夏寶庫" —— 陝西歷史博物館

○ 中國第一座現代化設施完備的大型博物館

○ 坐落在西安市南郊唐大雁塔西北1240米處

○ 館區佔地65000多平方米

○ 建築面積近60000平方米

○ 唐風館舍軸綫對稱,雄偉壯觀,古樸典雅

○ 1991年6月20日建成開館

○ 文物庫區面積近8000平方米,館藏文物370000多件

○ 展廳面積11600多平方米,展出文物2700多件

○ 本館科研工作重點

　　△ 周秦漢唐歷史文化研究

　　△ 館藏文物分類研究

　　△ 博物館學研究

　　△ 文物保護科學實驗

○ 爲觀衆服務的設施齊備

○ 開館以來接待觀衆200多萬人次

○ 日接待觀衆量最高達8000多人次

- Shaanxi History Museum — "Bright star of the ancient capital, cultural treasures of China".
- It is the first modernized museum with perfect installations in China.
- It is located in Xi'an's southern suburbs, about 1,240 meters northwest of the Big Wild Goose Pagoda.
- Its total area is about 65,000 square meters.
- The buildings cover a floor space about 60,000 square meters.
- The structure with architectural styles of the Tang Dynasty is grand and elegant, which represents the traditional Chinese aesthetic principle of "perfect symmetry with the axle line."
- The museum was formally opened to visitors on June 20, 1991.
- All of the storehouses cover a floor space of 8,000 square metres, and the relics collected here are more than 370,000 pieces.
- The exhibition halls occupy a total area of 11,600 square metres, and the exhibits are more than 2,700 pieces.
- The leading professional reseach work here are:
  - △ Historical and cultural studies on Zhou, Qin, Han and Tang Dynasties.
  - △ Classification studies of cultural relics.
  - △ Museology studies.
  - △ Cultural relics protection and scientific experiments.
- For serving visitors, the museum is well appointed.
- Since June 20, 1991, the number of visitors is 2,000,000.
- The maximum number of visitors in a day is about 8,000.

沿革
Development

○1944年6月，前陝西省府在西安碑林內設立陝西省歷史博物館
○1949年5月，陝甘寧邊區政府接收了陝西省歷史博物館
○1950年5月，改名為西北歷史文物陳列館
○1952年11月，改稱西北歷史博物館
○1953年3月，碑林前的孔廟被擴充為館區
○1953年7月，開始舉辦歷史陳列
○1955年6月，館名定為陝西省博物館

○1973年6月，周恩來總理來西安，視察陝西省博物館。指示："陝西文物很多，展室窄小。在適當的時候新建一個博物館。"
○1977年，陝西省文化局和陝西省博物館建議："碑林石刻原地調整，歷史陳列另建新館。"
○1978年3月，國家計委批復了陝西省革委會呈國務院《關於新建陝西省博物館的請示報告》，撥下建館專款。但因館址定不下來，使新館建設未能付諸實施
○1983年，確定了新建館的館址（即今址）
○1984年初，陝西省政府成立以省長為主任的陝西省歷史博物館籌建委員會
○1984年4月，西北建築工程咨詢公司完成了《陝西省歷史博物館新館工程咨詢報告》
○1984年6月，陝西省計委批復了《陝西省歷史博物館工程計劃任務書》
○1984年9月，新館建築初步設計方案的篩選審定工作結束
○1984年10月，文化部部長朱穆之指示："陝西省歷史博物館規模要大些，建築標準要提高。"
○1985年初，陝西省計委發出《關於變更陝西省歷史博物館建築規模的通知》
○1985年2月，陝西省歷史博物館籌建處正式組建

○1985年2～3月，陝西省文化文物廳副廳長陳全方等赴京，向中共中央書記處書記鄧力羣以及國家計委副主任房維中和文化部文物局局長呂濟民等領導滙報工作，要求把陝西省歷史博物館新館工程列入國家"七五"計劃。當場確定投資1.2億元

○截止1985年底，新館的陳列設計大網，展室文物庫房及其他建築設備的工藝資料，館區用地徵遷和建築擴初設計文件的編制等項工作陸續完成

○1986年1月17日，國家計委下達《關於陝西省新建陝西歷史博物館設計任務書的批復》，去掉了館名中的"省"字，確定了新建館的建築規模、標準和投資方案。批復明確指出："陝西歷史博物館是國家級博物館。"

○1986年3～4月，全國人大六屆四次會議通過的《中華人民共和國國民經濟和社會發展第七個五年計劃》把陝西歷史博物館新館工程列爲國家重點建設項目

○1986年8月，陝西歷史博物館籌建處的領導班子改組加強

○1986年11月28日，陝西歷史博物館新館工程破土奠基

○1987年7月1日，新館主體工程開始施工

○1988年，新館現代化配套設備的設計和訂貨工作基本結束

○1989～1990兩年，新館建築施工和設備安裝同步進行

○1991年初，陝西省文物局主持實施了陝西歷史博物館和碑林博物館的分館（包括人員和文物藏品）工作

○1991年4月16日，陝西省編委批復了陝西歷史博物館機構設置和人員編製方案，同意設置陳列部、保管部、宣教部和圖書資料室等業務部門。陝西歷史博物館籌建處同時撤銷

○1991年6月中旬，新館建築工程、館區環境整治和基本陳列、臨時展覽同時告竣

○1991年6月19日，任命了尹盛平（副館長主持全盤工作）、楊培鈞、韓偉、李偉、孫文定等五位館級領導

○1991年6月20日，陝西歷史博物館舉行盛大的開館典禮

○1992年7月17日，任命陳全方爲陝西歷史博物館館長

○June, 1944	Shaanxi Museum of History was set up by the former Government of Shaanxi Province in Xi'an Forest of Steles.
○May, 1949	The Museum was taken over by the Government of Shaanxi-Gansu-Ningxia Border Region.
○May, 1950	The Museum was named Northwestern Museum of Historical and Cultural Relics.
○November, 1952	The Museum was renamed Northwestern Museum of History.
○March, 1953	The Confucian Temple in front of the Forest of Steles was merged into the museum.
○July, 1953	Exhibitions began to be held on historical relics.
○June, 1955	The Museum was once again renamed. It was called the Museum of Shaanxi Province.

○June, 1973	The late Premier Zhou came to Xi'an and pointed out: "Xi'an is very rich in cultural relics, but the exhibition hall is too small, so a new and large one is needed, which should be built in proper time."
○1977	Shaanxi Cultural Bureau and the Museum of Shaanxi Province jointly proposed: "The stone carvings of the Forest of Steles should be housed where they are now. For the historical exhibits, a new museum should be set up."
○March, 1978	The State Planning Commission gave the approval reply to Shaanxi Revolutionary Committee on the "Application for the New Construction of Shaanxi Provincial Museum" submitted to the State Council, and allocated special funds for it. But because the location of the museum was not decided, the project did not come into effect.
○1983	The new site of the museum (today's site) was selected.
○Early in 1984	The Preparatory Committee for the Construction of Shaanxi Provincial History Museum was set up by the Shaanxi People's Government, with the governor as its director.
○April, 1984	"The Report on Advice-Seeking for the Project of the New Museum Construction" was finished by the Northwestern Architectural Consultation Company.

○June, 1984	"The Plan of Construction Project of Shaanxi Provincial History Museum" was approved by Shaanxi Planning Commission.
○September, 1984	The preliminary design-programmes of the new museum construction were worked out and the best one was selected.
○October, 1984	Zhu Muzhi, Minister of Culture, gave instructions: "The size of Shaanxi Provincial History Museum should be larger and the architectural standard should be higher than the original."
○Earlier 1985	Shaanxi Planning Commission issued "The Circular on the Expension of the Architectural Scale of Shaanxi Provincial History Museum."
○February, 1985	The Preparatory Office of Shaanxi Provincial History Museum was set up.
○February-March, 1985	The Bureau of Shaanxi Cultural Relics sent the high official Mr. Chen Quanfang and others to Beijing to report the construction project of the new Shaanxi Provincial History Museum to Secretary Deng Liqun of the Secretariat of Central Party Committee, Vice-director Fang Weizhong of the State Planning Commission and Director Lye Jiming of the Bureau of Cultural Relics of Ministry of Culture, asking them to list the construction project as an item to be carried out in the Seventh Five-Year Plan. And on the spot the leaders decided to invest 1.2 hundred million yuan for the new museum.
○At the end of 1985	The exhibition programme, the technological data for the construction of relics storehouse and other necessary buildings, and the expansion plan as well as the location of the new museum, all were gradually finished.

○January 17, 1986	The State Planning Commission gave its approval reply to "The Report on the Design and Project of the New Construction of Shaanxi Provincial History Museum" and the former word "provincial" was taken off. The reply clearly pointed out: "The Shaanxi History Museum is a state museum."
○March-April, 1986	In the Seventh Five-Year Plan for the National Economy and Social Development of the People's Republic of China adopted by the Fourth Session

of the Sixth People's Congress, the project of the construction of the new Shaanxi History Museum was listed as one of the leading items of national construction.

○August, 1986 — The leadership of the Preparatory Office of Shaanxi History Museum was strengthened.

○November 28, 1986 — The new museum laid its foundation stone of the construction.

○July 1, 1987 — The principal part of the new museum began its construction.

○1988 — The design was finished for the modernization of the new museum, and the orders were made for buying the complete sets of equipment.

○1989-1990 — The construction of the new museum and its installation of equipment were being carried simultaneously.

○Earlier 1991 — The division of Shaanxi History Museum from the Forest of Steles (including cultural relics and staff members) was made under the guidance of the Bureau of Shaanxi Cultural Relics.

○April 16, 1991 — Shaanxi Staff and Organization Commission authorized the Museum as an independent institution and the number of its staff members. And some of the professional departments, such as the Displaying Department, Cultural Relics Preservation and Repairing Department, Reception Organization and the Library were set up. At the same time the Preparatory Office was removed.

○In the middle of June, 1991 — The construction of the new museum, the beautification of its surroudings and the preparations for the exhibits display were all accomplished at the same time.

○June 19, 1991 — Mr. Yin Shengping was appointed to be the Party Secretary and deputy-curator of the museum and other four persons to be the leading officials, include Mr. Yang Peijun, Mr. Han Wei, Mr. Li Wei, and Mr. Sun Wending.

○June 20, 1991 — A grand opening ceremony of Shaanxi History Museum was held.

○July 17, 1992 — Mr. Chen Quanfang was appointed to be the curator of Shaanxi History Museum.

中華人民共和國主席江澤民參觀陝西歷史博物館（1993年6月12日）
Chairman Jiang Zemin visited the Museum on June 12, 1993.

日本國明仁天皇和
皇后美智子參觀陝西歷
史博物館
（1992年10月26日）
Emperor Akihito
and Empress Michiko
visited the Museum on
October 26, 1992.

國家前任主席楊尚昆在貴賓接待室題詞
Former chairman Yang Shangkun gives his inscription for the museum at the guest room.

聯合國教科文組織總幹事馬約爾參觀臨展
Mr. Mayor, general director of U.N.E.S.C.O., visits the temporary exhibitions.

朱鎔基副總理在唐代展廳參觀
Vice-Premier Zhu Rongji visits the Tang Dynasty Exhibition Hall.

美國前總統布什參觀陝西歷史博物館
Former U.S. President Bush visits the museum.

建築設備
Structure & Equipments

明快典雅的建築格調
> 深灰色的琉璃瓦屋面
> 乳白色的面磚牆面
> 古銅色的鋁合金型材鑲茶色玻璃門窗

The architectural hue of the buildings is sprightly and refined
> The deep grey glazed-tile housetop.
> The milky color brick wall.
> The dark brown glass door and window inlaid with
> the bronze-colored frames made of the aluminum alloy material.

館標集字 著名文豪郭沫若的手迹
The name "陝西歷史博物館" (Shaanxi History Museum) is collected the famous Chinese literary giant Guo Moruo's handicraft.

建築功能分區圖
Function map.

開放區域：展廳、接待室和
　　　　　商品部
收藏區域：文物庫、圖書樓
工作區域：業務研究、行政
　　　　　管理
設備用房：空調機房、變配
　　　　　電站等

The open area
　　Exhibition hall,
　　reception room and
　　shop.
The storage area
　　Storehouse, data
　　building.
The working area
　　Professional research
　　and administration.
The equipment area
　　Air-conditioner centre
　　and the electricity
　　control centre.

收藏區域
The Storage Area

工作區域
The Working Area

開放區域
The Open Area

設備用房
Equipment Room

地下室
Ground Room

文保中心
The Cultural Relics
Protecting Centre

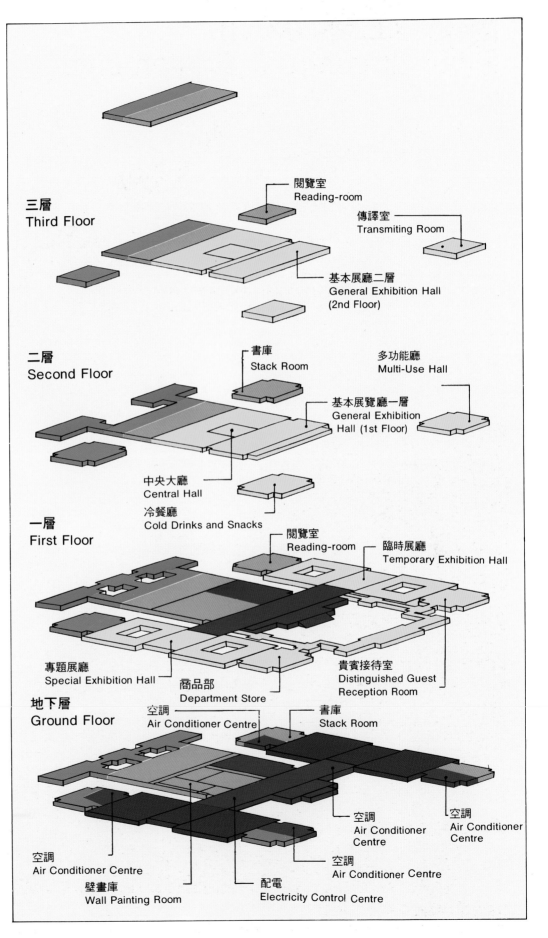

三層
Third Floor

閱覽室
Reading-room

傳譯室
Transmiting Room

基本展廳二層
General Exhibition Hall
(2nd Floor)

二層
Second Floor

書庫
Stack Room

多功能廳
Multi-Use Hall

基本展覽廳一層
General Exhibition
Hall (1st Floor)

中央大廳
Central Hall

冷餐廳
Cold Drinks and Snacks

一層
First Floor

閱覽室
Reading-room

臨時展廳
Temporary Exhibition Hall

專題展廳
Special Exhibition Hall

商品部
Department Store

貴賓接待室
Distinguished Guest
Reception Room

地下層
Ground Floor

空調
Air Conditioner Centre

書庫
Stack Room

空調
Air Conditioner
Centre

空調
Air Conditioner
Centre

空調
Air Conditioner Centre

空調
Air Conditioner Centre

壁畫庫
Wall Painting Room

配電
Electricity Control Centre

李鐵映視察館舍建築
Mr. Li Teiying inspects the museum construction.

館舍連廊
　　中央殿堂四隅崇樓通過連廊結合在一
The winding passage.
　　The overall layout of the buildings l
like a palace with halls in the centre
elegant pavilions standing in the fou
corners.

前庭院與主體建築
The front courtyard and the main structure.

寧靜肅穆的正門
The front gate, quiet
and solemn.

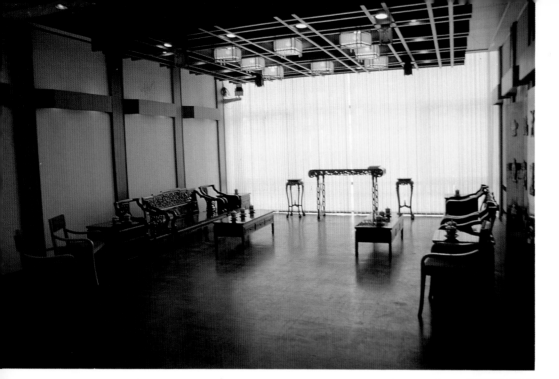

貴賓接待室
The guest room.

外賓服務部內景
The interior view of the foreign guest building.

多功能報告廳
裝置有六種語言的同聲傳譯系統和影視幻燈放映設備
The multi-function hall.
It provides six kinds of language translation systems and slide showing equipments.

電子計算機房
The computer room

空調機房
Air-conditioner center.

電話總機房
The telephone room.

變配電站
Electricity control
centre.

壁畫庫
　　當今一流水平，具有修復、保存和觀賞三重功能
The fresco preservation room.
　　It has three functions: repairing, preserving and appreciation.

李瑞環、馬文瑞等參觀
Mr. Li Ruihuan and M

i visit the fresco room.

書庫
The stack room.

圖書資料樓設計藏書量爲30萬册
編製有多種檢索系統
The capacity of storage is 300,000 copies.
The stack room is installed with programmed searching systems.

窗明几淨的閱覽室
The Reading Room —— bright and clean.

書庫
The stack room.

鄧力羣視察安全設施
Mr. Deng Liqun inspects the security center.

音像室
The video room.

陳列展覽
Exhibition Halls

展示文物考古成果的窗口
國內外文化交流的良好場所
The window for displaying cultural relics and archeaological
achievements all over the Shaanxi Province.
The appropriate place for making cultural exchanges between
China and other countries.

展廳外觀
External view of the exhibition hall.

舒適典雅的歷史文化殿堂
The elegant and confortable palace of history and culture.

泰國僧王頌錄拍央訕旺來陝西歷史博物館參觀
Tailand Buddhist king visited the museum.

銜接展廳的休息長廊
The long corridor connects each hall.

以色列總統赫爾佐格和夫人參觀陝西歷史博物館
Israil president Herzog visited the museum.

咨詢台
Consulting service.

停車場
Parking place.

《國際博物館協會憲章》強調爲
殘疾人服務，陝西歷史博物館
設有供殘疾人使用的電梯
Elevator for the handicaped.
According to the International
Museums Society Charter, the
museum provides the elevators
for the handicaped.

序言大廳
The introductory hall.

黃河，黃土，中華文明的源頭之一
順陵石獅，唐代文化高度發展的標誌

Yellow River, Yellow Land, craddle of Chinese civilization.
Stone lion (reproduced from Shunling, the tomb of China's first Empress Wu Zetian's mother), the sign of high cultural development of the Tang Dynasty.

展綫示意圖
Tourist Map of the Exhibitions.

展綫總長2300米，走向以中心序廳爲樞紐，呈點綫結合狀
The exhibition line is 2,300 meters long, running around the Central Hall.

● 館內標誌
Marks in the Hall

諮詢台
Consulting Counter

寄存處
Checkroom

厠所
Washingroom

公用電話
Telephone

冷餐廳
Cold Drinks and Snacks

商品部
Department Store

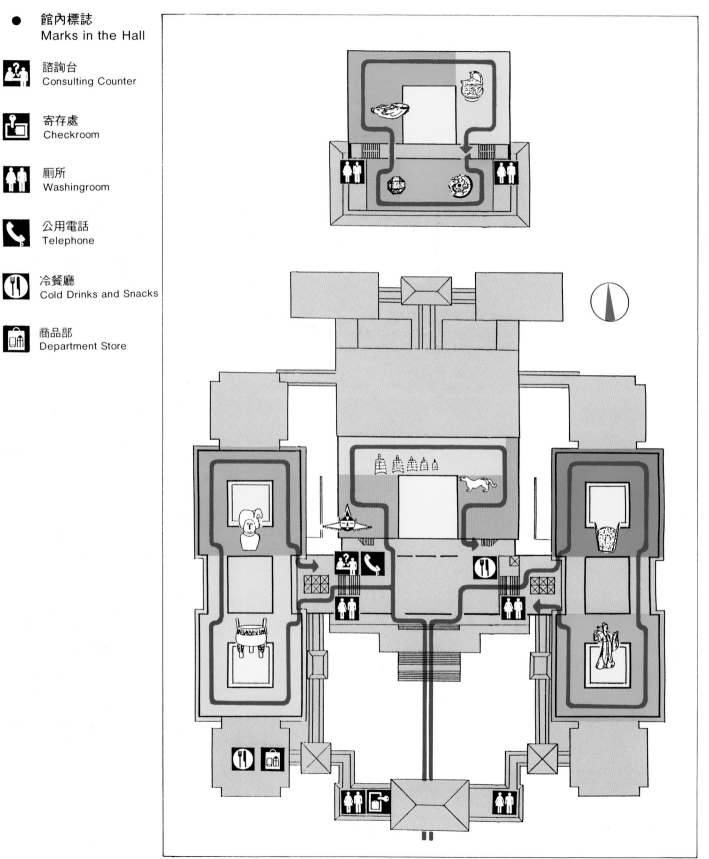

陳列展覽體系
以陝西古代史陳列爲主
以專題展覽爲輔
以臨時展覽爲補充
科學性、藝術性和通俗性相統一，格調高雅，雅俗共賞
Exhibition System:
The main exhibition is on the Shaanxi's ancient history from
prehistorial age to the Qing Dynasty.
Besides, there are Special and Temporary exhibitions, both of
them are supplementary exhibitions.
An elegant style is unified with science, artistry and popularization,
suitable to both refined and popular tastes.

陝西古代史陳列
展示三秦大地的昔日概貌
重點突出周秦漢唐光輝燦爛的物質文明
The Exhibition of the Ancient History of Shaanxi.
Generally showing the ancient appearance of Shaanxi (also
called Three Qin).
Especially stressing the fine material civilization of
Zhou, Qin, Han and Tang Dynasties.

周

周展廳
Zhou Dynasty
Exhibition Hall.

漢

漢展廳
Han Dynasty
Exhibition Hall.

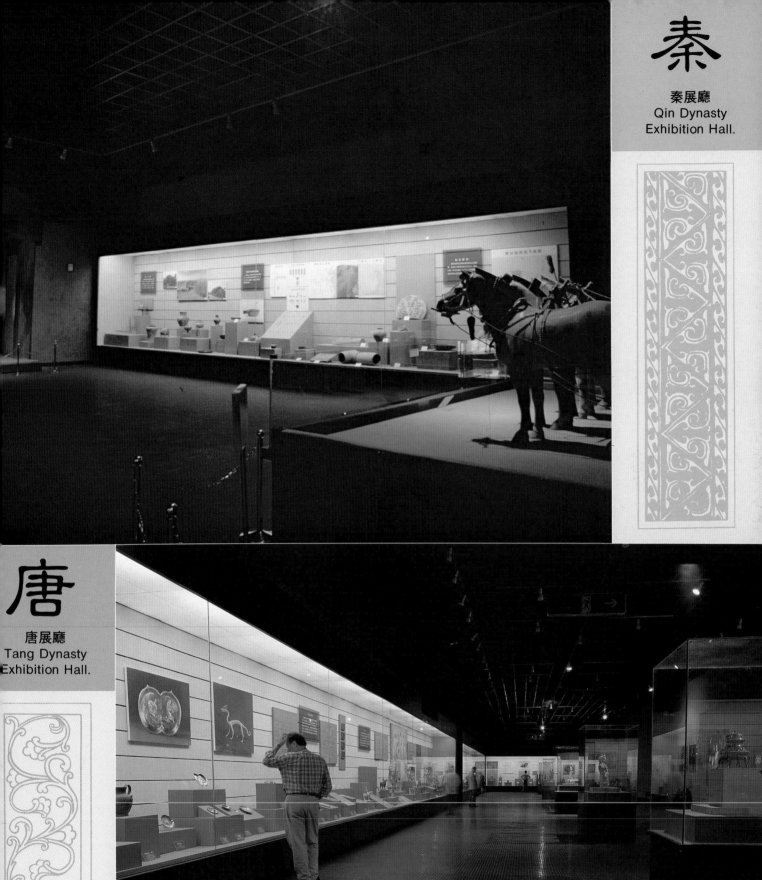

秦

秦展廳
Qin Dynasty
Exhibition Hall.

唐

唐展廳
Tang Dynasty
Exhibition Hall.

秦展廳
Qin Dynasty
Exhibition Hall.

日己觥　盛酒器
　　西周中期（公元前10－前9世紀）
　　通高32厘米
　　1963年陝西扶風出土
Ri Ji Gong, a wine container.
　　The Mid-Western Zhou Dynasty
　　(10th-9th century B.C.)
　　H. 32 cm.
　　Unearthed in 1963 at Fufeng
　　County, Shaanxi.

陝西青銅器珍品展
　　再現上古的神秘殿堂
The Exhibition of the Shaanxi Bronzes Treasures.
　　Precious bronzes represent the mystic palace of ancient times.

陝西歷代陶俑精華展
　　古代陶塑藝術長廊
The Pottery Gems Exhibition of Shaanxi in the Past Dynasties.
　　The long corridor of the ancient pottery sculpture arts.

唐墓壁畫眞品展覽
　盛唐社會風貌圖卷
The Exhibition of the Original Murals from the Tang Mausoleums.
　The painting scolls featuring the society of the Tang Dynasty in its prime.

蘇思勗墓玄武圖
　高188.5厘米，寬175厘米
　1952年出土於陝西西安
The Sombre Tortoise and Snake from the tomb of Su Sixu (670-745).
　H. 188.5cm, W. 175cm.
　Unearthed in 1952 at Xi'an, Shaanxi.

昭陵文物精品展覽

陝西地縣館藏精品集中展示

1991年6月－12月展出

The Exhibition of the Selected Cultural Relics from Zhaoling
(Mausoleum of the Tang Emperor Tai Zong).

Precious selected exhibits from the localities and counties.

They were exhibited here from June to December in 1991.

遼陳國公主墓文物展 (1992. 1. —— 1993. 8.)
　草原文化奇葩
The Cultural Relics Exhibition from the Tomb of Princess Chen Guo
of the Liao Dynasty (916-1125A.D.). Exhibited from January 1992 to August 1993.
　An exotic flower of grassland.

藏品精選 Selected Treasures

西周蟬紋鼎
Cauldron, a cooking vessel, designed with cicada patterns of the Western Zhou Dynasty

北朝漢白玉佛龕
White marble Buddhist shrine of the Northern Dynasties

藏 品 精 選
Selected Treasures

銅　　　　　器
金　銀　玉　器
唐　墓　壁　畫
陶　　　　　俑
貨　　　　　幣
陶　瓷　玻　璃
秦　漢　磚　瓦
漢　唐　銅　鏡

Bronzes
Gold, Silver and Jade Wares
Tang Dynasty Tomb Frescoes
Pottery Figures
Coins
Porcelains and Glasses
Bricks and Eave Tiles of the Qin-Han Dynasties
Bronze Mirrors of the Han and Tang Dynasties

鳥蓋瓠壺　盛酒器
　　　戰國（公元前475－221年）
　　　通高37.5厘米，口徑5.8厘米
　　　1967年陝西綏德出土
Gourd-shaped pot with a bird-shaped lid.
　　　Warring States period (475-221 B.C.)
　　　H.37.5cm., D. of mouth 5.8cm.
　　　Unearthed in 1967 at Suide County, Shaanxi.

蛙紋鉞　兵器
　　晚商（公元前13－前11世紀）
　　長20厘米
　　陝西城固出土
　　王權的象徵

Yue, an axe-like weapon, with frog pattern.
The Late Shang Dynasty (13th-11th century B.C.)
H.22 cm.
Unearthed from the Chenggu County, Shaanxi.
It's the symbol of the royal authority.

柞鐘　樂器
　　西周晚期（公元前9－前8世紀）
　　高11－23厘米
　　1960年陝西扶風出土
　　鐘鳴鼎食，商周貴族
　　生活氣象的再現

Zha bells, musical instruments.
The Late Western Zhou Dynasty (9th-8th century B.C.)
H.11-23cm.
Unearthed in 1960 at the Fufeng County, Shaanxi.
The bells before our eyes mirror the luxurious life
of the nobles in the Shang and Zhou Dynasties.

外叔鼎　烹飪器
　　西周晚期（公元前9－前8世紀）
　　通高89厘米，口徑61.3厘米
　　1952年陝西岐山出土
Wai Shu caldron, a cooking vessel.
　　The Late Western Zhou Dynasty (9th–8th century B.C.)
　　H.89 cm., D. of mouth 61.3 cm.
　　Unearthed in 1952 at the Qishan County, Shaanxi.

四足鬲　烹飪器
　　晚商（公元前13－前11世紀）
　　通高23.5厘米，口徑21厘米
　　陝西城固出土
　　全國獨一無二的精品
Li, a cooking vessel, with four legs.
　　The Late Shang Dynasty (13th-11th century B.C.)
　　H.23.5 cm., D. of mouth 21cm.
　　Unearthed from the Chenggu County, Shaanxi.
　　It's the unique treasure in China.

鳳柱斝　盛酒器
　　晚商（公元前13－前11世紀）
　　通高41厘米，口徑19.5厘米
　　1973年陝西岐山出土
Jia, a wine vessel, with a mouth of double-phoenix-pillar relief.
　　The Late Shang Dynasty (13th-11th century B.C.)
　　H.41 cm., D. of mouth 19.5 cm.
　　Unearthed in 1973 at Qishan County, Shaanxi.

牛形尊　盛酒器
　　西周中期（公元前10－前9世紀）
　　通高24厘米，長38厘米
　　1967年陝西岐山出土
Ox-shaped Zun, a wine vessel.
　　The Mid-Western Zhou Dynasty
　　(10th- 9th century B.C.)
　　H.24 cm., L.38 cm.,
　　Unearthed in 1961 at Qishan County, Shaanxi.

錐足饕餮紋鼎　烹飪器
　　晚商（公元前13－前11世紀）
　　高19厘米，口徑15厘米
　　陝西銅川出土
　　饕餮爲古代傳說中的怪獸，
　　貪吃曰饕，貪財曰餮
Caldron with Tao Tie designs.
　　The Late Shang Dynasty
　　(13th-11th century B.C.)
　　H.19 cm., D. of mouth 15 cm.
　　Unearthed from the Tongchuan County,
　　Shaanxi.
　　Tao Tie are the ancient mythical ferocious
　　animals. Tao greedy for food and Tie for
　　wealth.

提梁卣　盛酒器
晚商（公元前13－前11世紀）
通高36厘米，口14.8×11.6厘米
1971年陝西涇陽出土

You, a wine vessel, with a loop handle.
The Late Shang Dynasty
(13th-11th century B.C.)
H.36 cm., Mouth 14.8×11.6 cm.
Unearthed in 1971 at Jingyang County,
Shaanxi.

孟簋　食器
　　西周初年（公元前11－10世紀）
　　通高24.5厘米，口徑23.4厘米
　　1961年陝西長安出土
Meng Gui, a cooking vessel.
　　The Early Western Zhou Dynasty
　　(11th-10th century B.C.)
　　H.24.5 cm., D. of mouth 23.4 cm.
　　Unearthed in 1961 at the Chang'an
County, Shaanxi.

它盉

西周晚期（公元前9－前8世紀）

通高37.5厘米

1963年陝西扶風出土

盉是調酒用的器具，早期亦用來盛水

Ta He, a wine vessel.

The Late Western Zhou Dynasty
(9th-8th century B.C.)

H.37.5 cm.

Unearthed in 1963 at Fufeng County, Shaanxi.

"He" was used for mixing wine, and originally
for holding water.

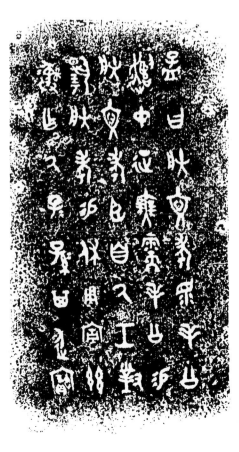

孟簋銘文拓片

The Meng Gui Inscription.

盠方彝　盛酒器
　　西周中晚期（公元前9世紀）
　　通高18厘米，口8.4×11.6厘米
　　1955年陝西眉縣出土
　　**銘文記載：周王命盠掌管西六師。還提到周王參加執
駒典禮的事**
Li Fang Yi, a wine vessel.
　　The Mid-late Western Zhou Dynasty (9th century B.C.)
　　H.18 cm., Mouth 8.4×11.6 cm.
　　Unearthed in 1955 at Meixian County, Shaanxi.
The inscriptions on it describe that the King of the Zhou
order Li to be in charge of "western six armies". And also
recorded the King jointed the ceremony of the "Zhi Ju"
(which was the ceremony for castrating the growing up
horses).

盠方彝銘文拓片
Li Fang Yi Inscription.

長劍
　　秦（公元前221年－207年）
　　通長91厘米，刃寬3.3厘米
　　1974年陝西臨潼秦始皇陵一號兵馬俑坑出土
Sword.
　　Qin Dynasty (221-207 B.C.)
　　L.91 cm., W. of the edge 3.3 cm.
　　Unearthed in 1974 at the No.1 Pit of Qinshihuang's
　　Mausoleum,
　　Lintong County, Shaanxi.

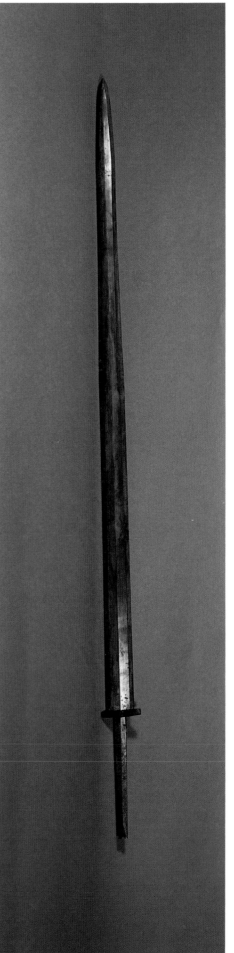

杜虎符
　　戰國（公元前475－221年）
　　高4.4厘米，長9.5厘米，厚0.7厘米
　　1973年陝西西安出土
　　虎符是古代調兵的信物
Tiger-shaped tally with characters of "杜" (Du), etc..
　　The Warring States period (475-221 B.C.)
　　H.4.4 cm., L.9.5 cm., Thickness 0.7 cm.
　　Unearthed in 1973 at Xi'an, Shaanxi.
It's a token used by emperor to confer military power
on ministers.

獅虎相鬥銅飾牌
　　西漢（公元前206－公元8年）
　　長10.5厘米，寬5.7厘米
　　館舊藏
Bronze ornament with fighting-lion-and-tiger design.
　　Western Han Dynasty (206 B.C.-8 A.D.)
　　L.10.5 cm., W.5.7 cm.
　　Shaanxi History Museum Collection.

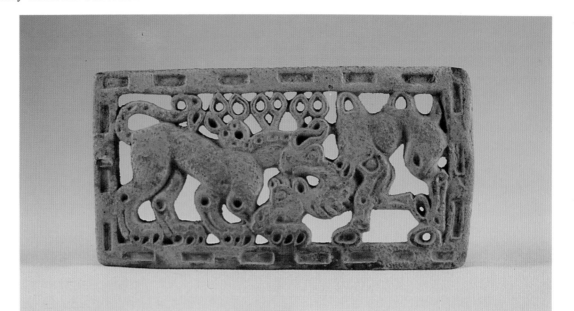

銅雁魚燈
　　西漢（公元前206年－公元8年）
　　通高54厘米，長33厘米，寬17厘米
　　1985年陝西神木出土
Bronze lamp in shape of a goose
having a fish in its mouth.
　　Western Han Dynasty
　　(206 B.C.-8 A.D.)
　　H.54 cm., L.33 cm., W.17 cm.
　　Unearthed in 1985 at Shenmu County,
　　Shaanxi .

金銀玉器
Gold, Silver and Jade Wares

八棱樂伎金杯　酒器
　　唐（618－907年）
　　高6.4厘米，口徑7.2厘米，重378克
　　1970年陝西西安出土
　　杯身八面各雕飾一伎樂人物，柄頂部雕兩相背人頭像，
　　造型別致
Gold octagonal cup with musicians and jugglers design,
a wine vessel.
　　Tang Dynasty (618-907 A.D.)
　　H.6.4 cm., D. of mouth 7.2 cm., W.378 gram.
　　Unearthed in 1970 at Xi'an, Shaanxi.
　　Each body of the cup carved with one figure. On the
top of the handle engraved with two human heads back
to back. The style is unique.

金啄木鳥
　　春秋・秦（公元前537年）
　　通高1.6厘米，通長1.5厘米
　　1986年陝西鳳翔出土
Gold wood-pecker, an ornament object.
　　Qin Kingdom of Spring and Autumn period (537 B.C.)
　　H.1.6 cm., L.1.5 cm.
　　Unearthed in 1986 at the No.1 Tomb of Gong Qin in
Fengxiang County, Shaanxi Province.

金狗
　　春秋・秦（公元前537年）
　　通高1.7厘米，通長3.5厘米
　　1986年陝西鳳翔出土
　　金啄木鳥和金狗，均爲陝西
　　最早的金製工藝品

Gold dog.
　　Qin Kingdom of Spring and Autumn period (537 B.C.)
　　H.1.7 cm., L.3.5 cm.
　　Unearthed in 1986 at the No.1 Tomb of Gong Qin in
Fengxiang County, Shaanxi Province.
The gold dog and the gold wood-pecker are the earliest
golden handicrafts in Shaanxi.

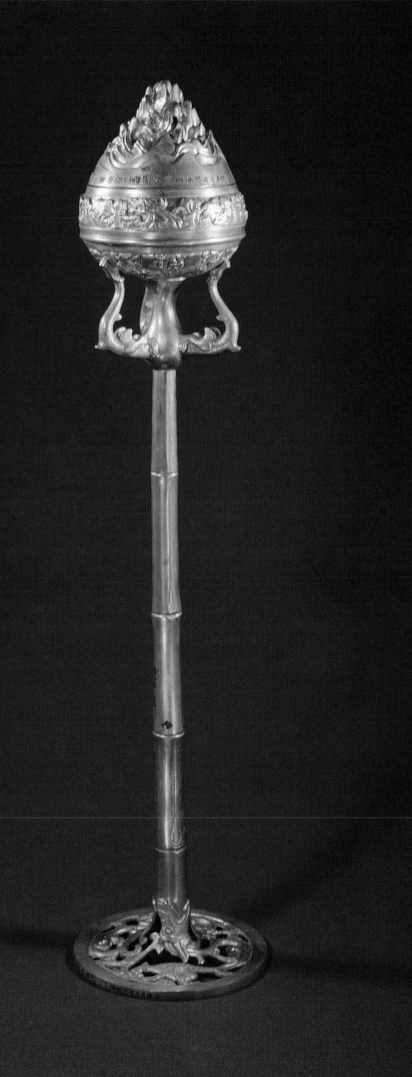

鎏金銀竹節銅熏爐
　　西漢中期（公元前153－前106年）
　　通高58厘米，底徑13.3厘米
　　1981年陝西茂陵出土
　　漢武帝姊陽信公主家的熏香用具
A gilt silver incense burner in the
form of bamboo joint.
　　Mid-Western Han Dynasty
　　(153-106 B.C.)
　　H.58 cm., D. of bottom 13.3 cm.
　　Unearthed in 1981 at Maoling
　　Mausoleum, Shaanxi.
　　It was a valuable article for daily
　　use of Princess Yangxin,
　　sister of Emperor Wudi in the
　　Han Dynasty.

金怪獸
漢（公元前206年－公元220年）
通長11厘米，高11.5厘米
1957年陝西神木出土
Gold deer-like animal.
Han Dynasty (206 B.C.-220 A.D.)
H.11.5 cm., L.11 cm.
Unearthed in 1957 at Shenmu County,
Shaanxi.

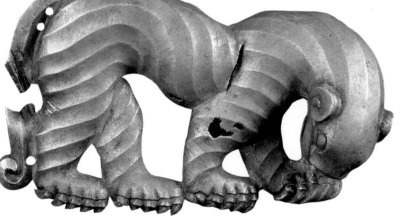

銀虎
漢（公元前206－公元220年）
高7厘米，長11厘米
1957年陝西神木出土
Silver tiger.
Han Dynasty (206 B.C.-220 A.D.)
H.7 cm., L.11 cm.
Unearthed in 1957 at Shenmu County,
Shaanxi.

銀鹿
漢（公元前206年－公元220年）
通高6.5厘米，長8.9厘米
1957年陝西神木出土
Silver deer.
Han Dynasty (206 B.C.-220 A.D.)
H.6.5 cm., L.8.9 cm.
Unearthed in 1957 at Shenmu County,
Shaanxi.

八瓣鎏金人物紋銀杯　酒器
　　唐（618－907年）
　　高5.5厘米，口徑9.2厘米
　　1970年陝西西安出土
Gilt octagonal silver cup with figure design.
　　Tang Dynasty (618-907 A.D.)
　　H.5.5 cm., D. of mouth 9.2 cm.
　　Unearthed in 1970 at Xi'an, Shaanxi.

掐絲團花金杯
　　唐（618－907年）
　　高5.9厘米
　　口徑6.8厘米
　　1970年陝西西安出土
Gold cup with posy
pattern.
　　Tang Dynasty
　　(618-907 A.D.)
　　H.5.9 cm., D. of
　　mouth 6.8 cm.
　　Unearthed in 1970 at
　　Xi'an, Shaanxi.

塞金獸首瑪瑙杯　酒器
　　唐（618－907年）
　　高6.5厘米，長15.6厘米
　　1970年陝西西安出土
　　舉世無雙的孤品，具有異域風采，中外文化交流的史證

Ox-head-shaped agate cup, a wine vessel.
Tang Dynasty (618-907 A.D)
H.6.5 cm., L.15.6 cm.
Unearthed in 1970 at Xi'an, Shaanxi.
The cup has an exotic style. It serves as the proof of the
cultural exchanges between China and abroad.

熊紋六瓣銀盤
　　唐（618－907年）
　　高1厘米，口徑13.4厘米
　　1970年陝西西安出土
Silver plate with bear design.
　　Tang Dynasty (618-907 A.D.)
　　H.1 cm., D. of mouth 13.4 cm.
　　Unearthed in1970 at Xi'an, Shaanxi.

蔓草雙鳳紋銀方盒
　　唐（618－907年）
　　高10厘米，長寬均11.8厘米
　　1970年陝西西安出土
Silver square box with double-phoenix
and plants design.
　　Tang Dynasty (618-907 A.D.)
　　H.10 cm., L.11.8 cm., W.11.8 cm.
　　Unearthed in 1970 at Xi'an, Shaanxi.

鎏金鏤空鴻雁球路紋銀籠子　茶具
唐（618－907年）
通高17.8厘米，重654克
1987年陝西扶風出土
法門寺地宮珍寶之一

Openwork silver cage with gilt swan-goose and lotus
design, tea ware.
　　Tang Dynasty (618-907 A.D.)
　　H.17.8 cm., Weight 654 gram.
　　Unearthed in 1987 in Famen Temple at Fufeng County,
Shaanxi .
　　The cage is for drying tea. It's one of the treasures
from the crypt of Famen Temple.

鎏金舞馬銜杯紋銀壺
唐（618－907年）
高18.5厘米，口徑2.2厘米
1970年陝西西安出土
唐代皇帝生辰慶典，馴馬起舞，銜杯祝壽

Silver pot with design of dancing horse holding a cup in its mouth.
Tang Dynasty (618-907 A.D.)
H.18.5 cm., D. of mouth 2.2 cm.
Unearthed in 1970 at Xi'an, Shaanxi.
In the Tang dynasty, the horses were trained to dance and hold cup for emperor's birthday celebration.

鎏金十字折枝花銀碟
　　唐（618－907年）
　　高1.9厘米，口徑10厘米
　　1987年陝西扶風出土
Silver plate with gilt posy and tree-twig pattern.
　　Tang Dynasty (618-907 A.D.)
　　H.1.9 cm., D. of mouth 10 cm.
　　Unearthed in 1987 at the Famen Temple, Fufeng
County, Shaanxi.

鎏金雙狐紋剖桃形銀盤
　　唐（618－907年）
　　高1.5厘米，口徑22.5厘米
　　1970年陝西西安出土
Gilt silver plate in double-peach shape and with
double-fox design.
　　Tang Dynasty (618-907 A.D.)
　　H.1.5 cm., D. of mouth 22.5 cm.
　　Unearthed in 1970 at Xi'an, Shaanxi.

玉人頭
　新石器時代（約1萬年－4千年前）
　高4.5厘米
　1976年陝西神木出土
Head-shaped jade carving.
　The Neolithic Age (About ten thousand years-4000 years
　ago).
　H.4.5 cm.
　Unearthed in 1976 at Shenmu County, Shaanxi.

玉琮　禮器
　西周（公元前11－前8世紀）
　通高20.1厘米，口徑9.2厘米
　1981年陝西長安出土
Jade Cong, a sacrificial object.
　Western Zhou Dynasty
　(11th-8th B.C.)
　H.20.1 cm., D. of mouth 9.2 cm.
　Unearthed in 1981 at Chang'an
　County, Shaanxi.

"皇后之璽"玉璽
　　漢初（公元前202－前170年）
　　高2厘米，長2.8厘米，寬2.8厘米
　　1968年陝西咸陽出土
　　在漢高祖長陵附近發現，是呂后生前的御用之寶
The empress' jade seal inscribed with "皇后之璽"
(Huang Hou Zhi Xi)
　　The Early Han Dynasty (202-170 B.C.)
　　H.2 cm., L.2.8 cm., W.2.8 cm.
　　Unearthed in 1968 at Xianyang City, Shaanxi.
　　It was found near the Changling, the mausoleum of Han Emperor
　　Gaozu. This seal was used by Empress Lyehou.

赤金走龍
　　唐（618－907年）
　　高2-2.8厘米，長4厘米
　　1970年陝西西安出土
　　小巧玲瓏的工藝精品

Gold dragons in running position.
Tang Dynasty (618-907 A.D.)
H.2-2.8 cm., L.4 cm.
Unearthed in 1970 at Xi'an, Shaanxi.
They are small and exquisite art treasure of handicrafts.

獨孤信煤精組印
　　西魏（535－557年）
　　高4.6厘米，寬4.35厘米，重75.7克
　　陝西旬陽出土
　　印章共24面，其中14個面上刻着官職、
稱謂等。是北朝文物的精品
General Dugu Xin's polyhedron-jetted seals.
Western Wei Period (535-557 A.D.)
H.4.6 cm., W.4.35 cm., Weight 75.7 gram.
Unearthed from Xunyang County, Shaanxi.
The seal has 24 sides, on the 14 sides of
which are inscribed the official titles, names,
etc.. It is one of the rare cultural relics of
the Northern Dynasties.

鉸接式鉚金白玉鐲
　　唐（618－907年）
　　直徑8厘米，厚2.1厘米
　　1970年陝西西安出土
　　唐代貴婦人的首飾
Gold-inlaid white jade bracelets.
Tang Dynasty (618-907 A.D.)
D.8 cm., Thickness 2.1 cm.
Unearthed in 1970 at Xi'an, Shaanxi.
It's the personal ornaments for the noble
women in Tang Dynasty.

唐墓壁畫
Tang Dynasty Tomb Frescoes

房陵公主墓托果盤侍女圖
（局部）
　　高175厘米，寬93厘米
　　1976年陝西富平出土
　　房陵公主（619－673
年），唐高祖李淵的第
六女
Waiting maid with fruit tray
(Detail).
　　H.175 cm., W.93 cm.
　　Unearthed in 1976 at
Fuping County,
Shaanxi.
　　Princess Fang Ling
(619-673), the sixth
daughter of Li Yuan,
Emperor Gao Zu of the
Tang Dynasty.

房陵公主墓托盤提壺侍女圖
　　高175厘米，寬93厘米
　　1976年陝西富平出土
Waiting maid in men's wear
with a tray and pot.
　　H.175 cm., W.93 cm.
　　Unearthed from the tomb
of Princess Fang Ling,
Fuping County, Shaanxi.

李爽墓吹簫樂伎圖

　　高183.5厘米，寬92厘米

　　1956年陝西西安出土

A Woman Musician Playing Xiao (a Chinese vertical bamboo flute) From Tomb of Li Shuang

　　H: 183.5cm　W: 92cm

　　Unearthed in 1956 at the Xi'an City, Shaanxi

李壽墓整裝待行圖

　　高196.5厘米，寬131.5厘米

　　1973年陝西三原出土

　　李壽（577－630年），字神通，唐高祖李淵的堂弟

Waiting for setting out.

　　H.196.5 cm., W.131.5 cm.

　　Unearthed in 1973 at the tomb of Li Shou, Sanyuan County, Shaanxi.

　　Li Shou (577-630), also named Shentong, was the cousin of Li Yuan,

　　Tang Emperor Gaozu.

章懷太子墓儀衛領班圖
　　高195厘米，寬69.5厘米
　　1971年陝西乾縣出土
　　章懷太子李賢（665－684年），唐高宗李治第六子。被母武則天逼迫致死。706年陪葬乾陵

A leader of the guard of honour.
　　H.195 cm., W.69.5 cm.
　　Unearthed in 1971 at Qianxian County, Shaanxi.
　　Li Xian (665-684) was the sixth son of Li Zhi, Tang Emperor Gao Zong.
　　He was killed by his mother Wu Zetian when he was thirty-two years old. Till 706 A.D., Li Xian was honored with the title Crown Prince Zhang Huai by the Emperor Zhong Zong and was buried in Qianling Mausoleum.

永泰公主墓宮女圖
　　高176厘米，寬196.5厘米
　　1960年陝西乾縣出土
　　圖中亭亭玉立的持杯宮女，是盛唐少女的典型形象
　　永泰公主李仙蕙（684－701年），武則天的孫女，被祖母
　　毒死，706年陪葬乾陵

Maids of honour.
　　H.176 cm., W.196.5 cm.
　　Unearthed in 1960 from the tomb of Princess Yong Tai,
　　Qianling Mausoleum, Shaanxi.
　　The maid with a long-stemmed cup in her hands looks
　　pretty, slim and graceful, and has vivid facial expressions.
　　She was the typical girl of the Tang Dynasty.
　　Princess Yong Tai, named Li Xianhui (684-701), was the
　　granddaughter of Empress Wu Zetian. She was killed by
　　her
　　grandmother. Till 706 A.D., Princess Yong Tai was
　　accompanied burying in Qianling Mausoleum.

懿德太子墓闕樓圖

　　高280厘米，寬280厘米

　　1971年陝西乾縣出土

　　懿德太子李重潤（682－701年），唐中宗李顯的長子，被祖母武則天杖殺。706年陪葬乾陵

Palaces and watchtowers.

　　H.280 cm., W.280 cm.

　　From the tomb of Prince Yi De, Qianling Musoleum, Shaanxi.

　　Li Chongrun (682-701) was the first son of Li Xian, Tang Emperor Zhong Zong. He was beaten to death with a stick by Wu Zetian's order. Upon Emperor Zhong Zong's succession to the throne, Li Chongrun was honored with two posthumous titles: Crown Prince and Li the Virtuous. Till 706 A.D., he was accompanied burying in Qianling Mausoleum.

懿德太子墓宮女圖
　　高176厘米，寬115厘米
　　1971年陝西乾縣出土
　　未完成的佳作，勾勒的綫稿尚清晰可見
Maids of honour.
　　H.176 cm., W.115 cm.
　　Unearthed in 1971 at the tomb of Prince Yi De, Qianling
　　Mausoleum, Shaanxi.
　　We can clearly see the sketch lines in the picture and
　　the
　　colours are not finished yet. It provides valuable data for
　　the research of the painting skill in Tang Frescoes.

章懷太子墓馬毬圖⑴
　　高196厘米，寬154厘米
　　1971年陝西乾縣出土
　　馬毬是古代西亞傳入東土的一種體育運動，在唐代貴族
　　社會中尤爲盛行
Playing polo (Ⅰ).
　　H.196 cm., W.154 cm.
　　From the tomb of Li Xian, Qianling Mausoleum, Shaanxi.
　　Polo was a kind of sports introduced into China from
　　West Asia in ancient times. This game was very popular
　　in the noble society during the Tang Dynasty.

章懷太子墓馬毬圖⑵
　　高225厘米，寬156厘米
　　1971年陝西乾縣出土
Playing polo (Ⅱ)
　　H.225 cm., W.156 cm.
　　From the tomb of Li Xian, Qianling Mausoleum, Shaanxi.

章懷太子墓禮賓圖
　　高184.5厘米，長252.5厘米
　　1971年陝西乾縣出土
　　**東羅馬和高句麗等國使者
　　訪問大唐的寫眞**
Receiving foreign guests
　　H.184.5 cm., W.252.5 cm.
　　From the tomb of Li Xian,
　　Qianling Mausoleum, Shaanxi.
　　The fresco gives a true
　　description of the friendly
　　relations
　　between the Tang Empire
　　and Korea and the Eastern
　　Roman Empire.

章懷太子墓狩獵出行圖（之一）
　　高174厘米，寬220厘米
　　1971年陝西乾縣出土
　　原圖高100－200厘米，全長890厘米，揭取時分割爲數
　　幅。整個畫面以青山和松林爲背景，狩獵者縱馬奔馳，
　　還有兩匹輜重駱駝

Out for hunting（Ⅰ）.
　　H.174 cm., W.220 cm.
　　From the tomb of Li Xian, Qianling Mausoleum, Shaanxi.
　　This fresco was originally about 100-200 cm. high and
　　890 cm. long. It was cut carefully into several pieces
　　when taken off the wall. Against the background of green
　　hills and pine woods, the hunters were running and two
　　camels loaded with their necessities bring up the rear.

陶俑
Pottery Figures

三彩女侍俑
　　唐（618－907年）
　　高43厘米
　　1959年陕西西安出土

Tri-coloured figure of a maid.
Tang Dynasty (618-907 A.D.)
H.43 cm.
Unearthed in 1959 at Xi'an, Shaanxi.

跪射俑
　　秦（公元前221－207年）
　　高120厘米
　　1974年陕西临潼秦始皇陵兵马俑一號坑出土

Pottery figure kneeling and shooting.
Qin Dynasty (221-207 B.C.)
H.120 cm.
Unearthed in 1974 at the No.1 pit of Qinshihuang's Mausoleum, Shaanxi.

楊家灣兵馬俑
　　漢初（公元前179－前141年）
　　通高69厘米，馬長55厘米
　　1965年陝西咸陽出土
Pottery warrior and horse.
　　The Early Han Dynasty (179-141 B.C.)
　　H.69 cm., L. of the horse　55 cm.
　　Unearthed in 1965 at Yangjiawan,
　　Xianyang City,　Shaanxi.

楊家灣兵馬俑羣
　　西漢步騎兵相結合的軍陣
Pottery warriors and horses.
It is showing the combination of the infantryman
and the cavalry in the Western Han Dynasty.

胡人俑
西魏（535－557年）
高14.9厘米
1984年陝西咸陽出土

Pottery figure of a minority nationality.
Western Wei Period (535-557 A.D.)
H.14.9 cm.
Unearthed in 1984 at Xianyang City, Shaanxi.

人面鎮墓獸
西魏（535－557年）
通高36厘米，通寬21厘米，通長26厘米
陝西漢中出土

Tomb-guarding animal with a human face design.
Western Wei Period (535-557 A.D.)
H.36 cm., W.21 cm., L.26 cm.
Unearthed from Hanzhong City, Shaanxi.

騎馬號角俑
　　北魏（386－534年）
　　通高39厘米，馬長36厘米
　　1953年陝西西安出土
Pottery figure blowing a
horn on horse-back.
　　Northern Wei Period
　　(386-534 A.D.)
　　H.39 cm., L. of the horse 36 cm.
　　Unearthed in 1953 at
　　Xi'an, Shaanxi.

舂米俑
　　南北朝（420－589年）
　　通高16.5厘米，通長19.5厘米
　　陝西西安出土
Grains husking figure.
　　Northern and Southern
　　Dynasties (420-589 A.D.)
　　H.16.5 cm., L.19.5 cm.
　　Unearthed from Xi'an, Shaanxi.

三彩鎮墓獸
　　唐（618－907年）
　　通高59厘米
　　陝西西安出土
Tri-coloured figurine of
a tomb-guarding animal.
　　Tang Dynasty (618-907 A.D.)
　　H.59 cm.
　　Unearthed from Xi'an, Shaanxi.

貼金彩繪武官俑
　　初唐（675年）
　　高72厘米。
　　1971年陝西禮泉張士貴墓出土
Pottery figure of military officer.
　　The Early Tang Dynasty (675 A.D.)
　　H.72 cm.
　　Unearthed in 1971 at the tomb of Zhang
　　Shigui, Liquan County, Shaanxi.

貼金彩繪文官俑
　　初唐（675年）
　　高69厘米
　　1971年陝西禮泉張士貴墓出土
Pottery figure of civilian official.
　　The Early Tang Dynasty (675 A.D.)
　　H.69 cm.
　　Unearthed in 1971 at the tomb of Zhang
　　Shigui, Liquan County, Shaanxi.

三彩女坐俑
　　唐（618－907年）
　　高47.3厘米
　　1955年陝西西安出土
　　展示"對鏡貼花黃"的佳麗風姿
Tri-coloured figure of a sitting woman.
　　Tang Dynasty (618-907 A.D.)
　　H.47.3 cm.
　　Unearthed in 1955 at Xi'an, Shaanxi.
　　It shows the beautiful girl is dressing smartly.

f

.D.)

aanxi.
he nobles' tombs.

彩繪笠帽女騎俑
　　唐（663年）
　　通高71厘米，長29厘米
　　1971年陝西禮泉鄭仁泰墓出土
　　唐代麗人行的生動寫照
Painted pottery figure of a equestrienne with a hat.
　　Tang Dynasty (663 A.D.)
　　H.71 cm., L.29cm.
　　Unearthed in 1971 at the tomb of Zheng Rentai, Liquan
　　County, Shaanxi.
　　The vivid portraiture of the beauty of Tang Dynasty.

說唱俑

　唐（公元618－907年）
　(1)說唱俑　　高23厘米
　(2)吹笙俑　　高18厘米
　(3)擊樂俑　　高17.5厘米
　1966年陝西西安出土

Pottery figures in performance.

　Tang Dynasty (618-907 A.D.)

　a. Figure in talking and singing.
　　H.23 cm.

　b. Figure in playing Sheng, a reed pipe wind instrument.
　　H.18 cm.

　c. Figure in beating.
　　H.17.5 cm.

　Unearthed in 1966 at Xi'an, Shaanxi.

相扑俑
　　金（1115－1234年）
　　高29.4-29.7厘米
　　1986年陕西渭南出土
　　怒目相视的竞技斗士
Pottery figures of wrestlers.
　　Kin Period(1115-1234 A.D.)
　　H.29.4-29.7 cm.
　　Unearthed in 1986 at Weinan City, Shaanxi.
　　The athletics men are glaring at each other.

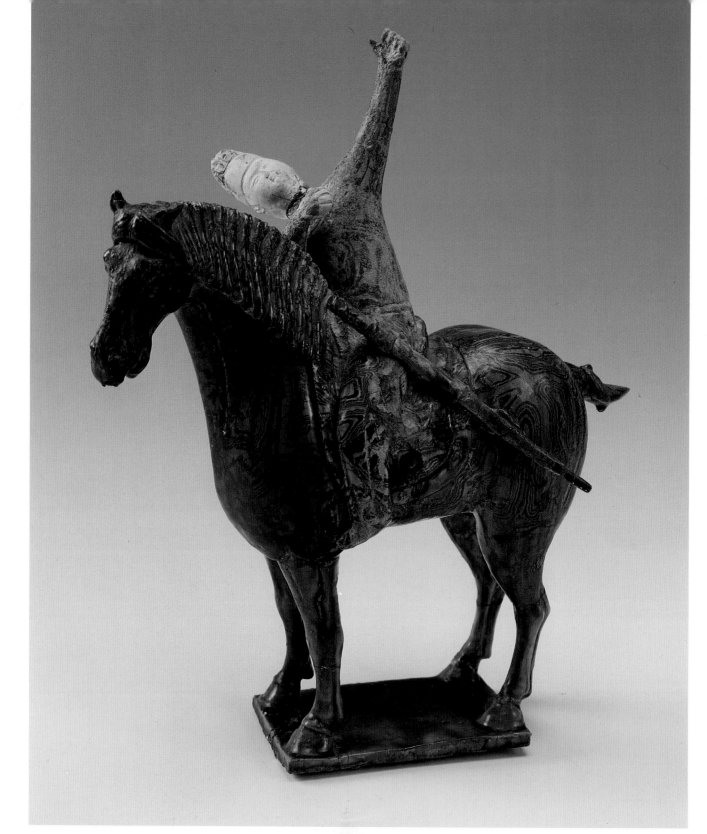

跨馬彎弓射雕俑
唐
通高36.2，長30厘米
1971年陝西乾縣懿德太子李重潤墓出。

Pottery figure riding and shooting.
Tang Dynasty (618－907 A.D.)
H. 36.2cm. L. 30cm.
Unearthed in 1972 at the tomb of Prince Yi De, Qianxian County, Shaanxi.

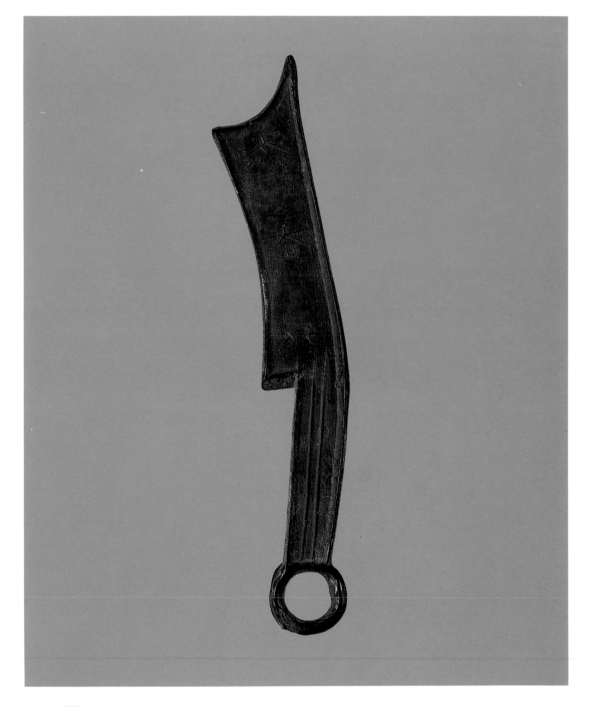

"齊法化"刀幣
　　戰國・齊（公元前386－前221年）
　　通長18.5厘米
　　館舊藏
Knife-shaped coin with the characters
of "齊法化" (Qi Fa Hua).
　　Qi Kingdom of Warring States period
　　(386-221 B.C.)
　　L.18.5 cm.
　　Shaanxi History Museum Collection.

"安邑二釿"布幣
　　戰國・魏（公元前403年－前225年）
　　通長6.6厘米
　　館舊藏
Shovel-shaped coin with characters
of "安邑二釿" (An Yi Er Jin).
　　Wei Kingdom of Warring States period
　　(403-225 B.C.)
　　L.6.6 cm.
　　Shaanxi History Museum Collection.

"郢爰"金幣
　　戰國・楚（公元前475－前223年）
　　長2.3厘米，寬1.8厘米
　　1964年陝西西安出土
Gold coin with the characters
of "郢爰" (Yin Yuan).
　　Chu Kingdom of Warring States period
　　(475-223 B.C.)
　　L.2.3 cm., W.1.8 cm.
　　Unearthed in 1964 at
　　Xi'an, Shaanxi.

玉五銖

西漢中晚期（公元前140－公元8年）

直徑2.3厘米

陝西寶鷄出土

Jade coin with the Chinese seal characters of "五銖" (Wu Zhu).

The Mid-late period of Western Han Dynasty (140 B.C.-8 A.D.)

D. 2.3cm.

Excavated from Baoji City, Shaanxi.

金五銖

西漢中晚期（公元前140－公元8年）

直徑2.5厘米

1980年陝西咸陽出土

Gold coin with the characters of "五銖" (Wu Zhu).

The Mid-late period of Western Han Dynasty (140 B.C.-8 A.D.)

D.2.5 cm.

Unearthed in 1980 at Xianyang City, Shaanxi.

馬蹄金
　西漢中晚期
　（公元前140－公元8年）
　長5.2厘米，高4.0厘米，
　寬6.0厘米，重246.4克
　1974年陝西西安出土
Taxation gold in the shape
of a horse-hoof.
　The Mid-late period of
　Western Han Dynasty
　(140 B.C.-8 A.D.)
　L.5.2 cm., H.4.0 cm.,
　W.6.0 cm., Weight 246.4 gram.
　Excavated from Xi'an
　in 1974, Shaanxi.

麟趾金
　西漢中晚期
　（公元前140－公元8年）
　直徑4.6厘米，厚2.5厘米，
　重261.9克
　1975年陝西西安出
　馬蹄形、麟趾形金塊，均爲
　西漢上等貨幣
Taxation gold in the shape
of a unicorn-hoof.
　The Mid-late period of Western H
　Dynasty (140 B.C.-8 A.D.)
　D.4.6 cm., Thickness 2.5 cm.,
　Weight 261.9 gram.
　Unearthed from Xi'an
　in 1975, Shaanxi.
　Unicorn-hoof and horse-hoof
　gold are the superior coins
　in the Han Dynasty.

"開元通寶"金幣
　　唐（618－907年）
　　直徑2.3厘米
　　1970年陝西西安出土
Gold coin with the characters of
"開元通寶" (Kai Yuan Tong Bao).
　　Tang Dynasty (618-907 A.C.)
　　D.2.3 cm.
　　Excavated from Xi'an, Shaanxi, 1970.

波斯銀幣⑴
　　波斯薩珊王朝庫思老二世（590－628年）
　　直徑3.1厘米
　　陝西西安出土
Silver coin of Persia (1)
　　Sasanian period of Persia (590-628 A.D.)
　　D.3.1 cm.
　　Excavated from Xi'an, Shaanxi.

波斯銀幣⑵
　　波斯薩珊王朝庫思老二世（590－628年）
　　直徑2.6厘米
　　陝西西安出土
Silver coin of Persia (2)
　　Sasanian period of Persia (590-628 A.D.)
　　D.2.6 cm.
　　Excavated from Xi'an, Shaanxi.

日本"和同開寶"銀幣
（日）奈良元明天皇時期（708－715年）
直徑2.4厘米
1970年陝西西安出土
唐代流傳到中國
Japanese silver coin with the characters of
"和同開寶" (He Tong Kai Bao).
(Japan) The Nara period (708-715 A.D.)
D.2.4 cm.
Excavated from Xi'an, Shaanxi, 1970.
It is the Japanese coin that was circulated
in China in the Tang Dynasty.

西域"高昌吉利"古幣
麴氏高昌國時期（500－640年）
直徑2.6厘米
1970年陝西西安出土
Ancient Western Area coin with the
characters of "高昌吉利" (Gao Chang Ji Li).
Qushi Gaochang period (500-640 A.D.)
D.2.6 cm.
Excavated from Xi'an in 1970, Shaanxi.
The Chinese characters of the "高昌吉利"
(Gao Chang Ji Li) was inscribed on this coin.

陶瓷玻璃
Porcelains and Glasses

彩陶獸面紋壺
　新石器時代（約1萬年－4千年前）
　高27.5厘米，底徑8厘米
　陝西臨潼出土
　圖案古拙，令人稱羨

Coloured pottery jar.
　The Neolithic Age
　(About 10-4 thousand years ago)
　H.27.5 cm., D. of bottom 8 cm.
　Unearthed from the Ruins of
　Jiangzhai, Lintong County,
　Shaanxi.
　The design is of primitive simplicity.

堆塑蟠螭紋陶罐
　新石器時代（約1萬年－4千年前）
　高15厘米，口徑18厘米
　陝西安塞出土
Pottery jar with
double-dragon patterns.
　The Neolithic Age
　(About 10-4 thousand years ago)
　H.15 cm., D. of mouth 18 cm.
　Unearthed from Ansai County, Shaanxi.

彩陶葫蘆瓶
　新石器時代（約1萬年－4千年前）
　高25.5厘米，底徑9厘米
　陝西臨潼出土
Coloured pottery jar.
　The Neolithic Age
　(About 10-4 thousand years ago)
　H.25.5 cm., D. of bottom 9 cm.
　Unearthed from the Ruins of
　Jiangzhai, Lintong County,
　Shaanxi.

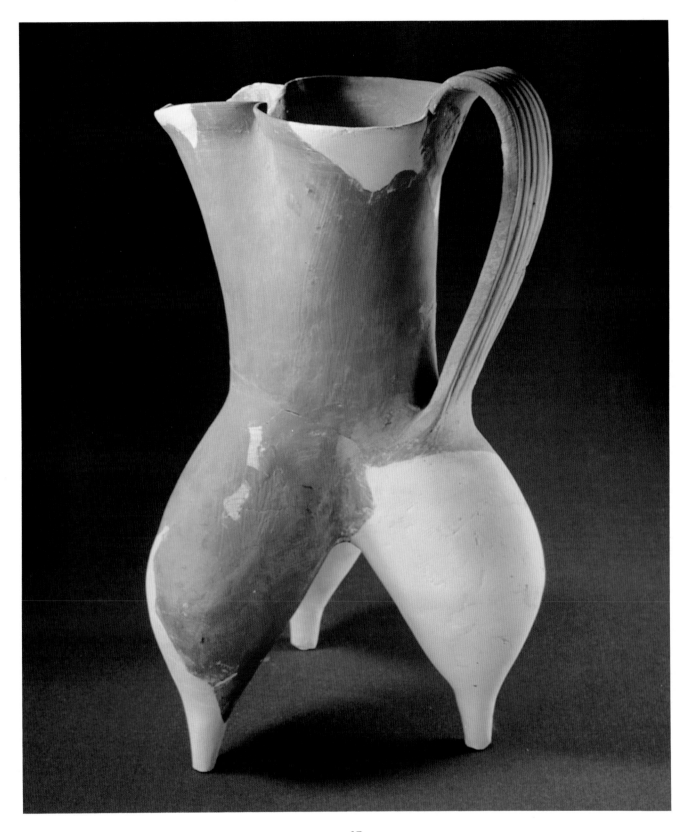

袋足白陶鬶

　　新石器時代（約1萬年－4千年前）

　　通高 28.5厘米

　　陝西臨潼出土

White pottery Gui, a cooking vessel, with pouch-shaped
legs.

　　The Neolithic Age (About 10-4 thousand years ago)

　　H.28.5 cm.

　　Unearthed from Lintong County, Shaanxi.

赭釉陶鐘
　　西漢（公元前206－公元8年）
　　通高25.5厘米，腹圍68厘米
　　館舊藏
Painted pottery "Zhong".
　　Western Han Dynasty (206 B.C.-8 A.D.)
　　H.25.5 cm., Belly perimeter 68 cm.
　　Shaanxi History Museum Collection.

青釉獅形注
　　北朝（386－581年）
　　通高11.8厘米，長17.5厘米
　　館舊藏
Green porcelain lion-shaped
water dropper.
　　The Northern Dynasties
　　(386-581 A.D.)
　　H.11.8 cm., L.17.5 cm.
　　Shaanxi History
　　Museum Collection.

藍玻璃盤
　　唐（618－907年）
　　直徑15.7厘米，高2.2厘米
　　1987年陝西扶風出土
　　唐代玻璃多從異域輸入，當時人極爲珍視
Blue glass plate.
　　Tang Dynasty (618-907 A.D.)
　　D.15.7 cm., H.2.2 cm.
　　Unearthed in 1987 at Famen Temple, Fufeng County,
　　Shaanxi.
　　During the Tang Dynasty, most of the glasses were
　　imported from
　　aboard, so they were very precious.

秘色瓷盤
　　唐（618－907年）
　　高6.8厘米，口徑22.4厘米
　　1987年陝西扶風出土
　　秘色瓷，唐代宮廷專用。燒制技術現已失傳

Olive green porcelain plate.
　　Tang Dynasty (618-907 A.D.)
　　H.6.8 cm., D. of mouth 22.4 cm.
　　Unearthed in 1987 at Famen Temple,
　　Fufeng County, Shaanxi.
The olive porcelain was used exclusively
for imperial palace.
The manufacturing technology
was missing.

白瓷蓮瓣碟
　　唐（618－907年）
　　高3.4厘米，口徑13.5厘米
　　陝西西安出土
Petal-shaped white china plate.
　　Tang Dynasty (618-907 A.D.)
　　H.3.4 cm., D. of mouth 13.5 cm.
　　Unearthed from Xi'an, Shaanxi.

青白釉雙龍柄瓷瓶
唐
通高51.3，口徑14，腹圍83厘米
本館舊藏

Celadonman-hold vase.
Tang Dynasty (618–907 A.D.)
H. 51.3cm. D. of mouth 14cm. D. of belly 83cm.
Shaanxi History Museum Collection.

娃娃枕
　　金（1115－1234年）
　　通高15.5厘米，通長44.5厘米
　　陝西黃陵出土
Pillow in the shape of a sleeping child.
　　Kin Period (1115-1234 A.D.)
　　H.15.5 cm., L.44.5 cm.
　　Unearthed from Huangling County, Shaanxi.

醬釉三魚紋扁壺
　　元（1271－1368年）
　　高30.6厘米，寬27.5厘米，厚9.5厘米
　　陝西韓城出土
Brown-glazed jar with three-fish patterns.
　　Yuan Dynasty (1271-1368 A.D.)
　　H.30.6 cm., W.27.5 cm., Thickness 9.5 cm.
　　Unearthed from Hancheng City, Shaanxi.

青釉倒注壺
宋（960－1279年）
高19厘米，底徑7.5厘米，腹徑14.3厘米
館舊藏
Green-glazed kettle with a bottom in-let.
Song Dynasty (960-1279 A.D.)
H.19 cm., D. of bottom 7.5 cm., D. of belly 14.3 cm.
Shaanxi History Museum Collection.

五彩饕餮紋瓷方鼎

　　明（1368－1644年）

　　高12.8厘米，口徑15.9×12.8厘米

　　1973年陝西綏德出土

Tripod with ogre-mask pattern.

　　Ming Dynasty (1368-1644 A.D.)

　　H.12.8 cm., D. of mouth 15.9×12.8 cm.

　　Unearthed in 1973 at Suide County, Shaanxi.

描金孔雀牡丹紋執壺
明（1368－1644年）
高29厘米，寬15厘米，厚9厘米
1959年陝西耀縣出土
Gold-traced jar with peacock and peony design.
Ming Dynasty (1368-1644 A.D.)
H.29 cm., W.15 cm., Thickness 9 cm.
Unearthed in 1959 at Yaoxian County, Shaanxi.

脱胎粉彩碗
　　清（1644－1911年）
　　高6.9厘米，口径13.2厘米
　　馆旧藏
Beautiful colored bowl with delicate design.
Qing Dynasty (1644-1911 A.D.)
H.6.9 cm., D. of mouth 13.2 cm.
Shaanxi History Museum Collection.

秦漢磚瓦

Bricks and Eave Tiles of
the Qin-Han Dynasties

夔鳳紋遮朽
秦（公元前221－前207年）
通高43厘米，面徑61厘米
陝西臨潼出土
遮朽是建築檁頭的遮蓋物，俗稱"瓦當王"

Big eave tile (Zhe Xiu).
Qin Dynasty (221-207 B.C.)
H.43 cm., D.61 cm.
Unearthed from Qinshihuang's Mausoleum.
Zhe Xiu were used as the covers put on the head of the purlin of the buildings, commonly called the king of tile-ends.

鹿紋瓦當
春秋·秦（公元前770－前476年）
面徑3.7厘米
1982年陝西鳳翔出土

Eave tile with deer design.
Qin Kingdom of the Spring and Autumn period (770-476 B.C.)
D.3.7 cm.
Unearthed from the Ruins of Yongcheng, Fengxiang County, Shaanxi.

鳥紋瓦當
春秋·秦（公元前770－前476年）
面徑4.5厘米
1982年陝西鳳翔出土

Eave tile with bird design.
Qin Kingdom of the Spring and Autumn period (770-476 B.C.)
D.4.5 cm.
Excavated from Fengxiang County in 1982, Shaanxi.

"右空"瓦當
　　西漢（公元前206－公元8年）
　　面徑15.7厘米
　　館藏
Eave tile with
 the characters of
"右空" (You Kong).
　　Western Han Dynasty
　　(206 B.C.-8 A.D.)
　　D.15.7 cm.
　　Shaanxi History
　　Museum Collection.

"延年益壽與天相持日月同光"磚
　　西漢（公元前206－公元8年）
　　長48.4厘米，寬10.5厘米
　　陝西西安出土
Brick with an auspicious Language.
　　Western Han Dynasty (206 B.C.-8 A.D.)
　　L.48.4cm, W.10.5cm.
　　Unearthed from Xi'an, Shaanxi.

紋瓦當（靑龍・白虎・朱雀・玄武）
西漢（公元前206－公元8年）
面徑19厘米
1956年陝西西安出土
靑龍、白虎、朱雀、玄武合稱四神，是
東、西、南、北四個方位的神祇形象
Four Patron Sainte eave tiles.
Western Han Dynasty (206 B.C.-8 A.D.)
D.19 cm.
Unearthed in 1956 at the Ruins
of Chang'an site of the
Han Dynasty, Shaanxi.
The green dragon, white tiger, red
scarlet bird and Xuan Wu are
mythologically called the four
patron saints. They defend
the four directions: the east,
west, south and north.

"車馬出行"畫像磚
漢
長40.5，寬47，厚5.8厘米
本館舊藏

Stone relief with marching chariots
and horses.
L. 40.5cm. W. 47cm. T. 5.8cm.
Han Dynasty (206 B.C.－220 A.D.)
Shaanxi History Museum Collection.

鋪首玉璧人物游龍追魚紋空心磚
漢
高27.5，寬52，厚12厘米
本館舊藏

Hollow brick in a design of human
and a dragon with fish pattern.
H. 27.5cm. W.52cm. T. 12cm.
Han Dynasty (206B.C.－220A.D.)
Shaanxi History Museum Collection.

陰刻龍紋空心磚
秦
殘長44.5，寬36，厚16厘米
本館舊藏

Hollow brick with dragon design.
Qin Dynasty (221－206 B.C.)
L. 44.5cm W. 36cm. T. 16cm.
Shaanxi History Museum Collection.

漢唐銅鏡

Bronze Mirrors of the Han
and Tang Dynasties

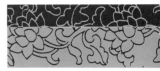

團龍紋鏡
唐（618－907）
直徑12厘米
館舊藏
Mirror with dragon
design.
　Tang Dynasty (618-907
A.D.)
D.12 cm.
Shaanxi History
Museum Collection.

四龍紋鏡
西漢（公元前206－公
元8年）
直徑20.7厘米
陝西安塞出土
Mirror with four-dragon
patterns.
　Western Han Dynasty
(206 B.C.-8 A.D.)
D.20.7 cm.
Excavated from
Ansai County, Shaanxi.

四獸紋鏡
西漢（公元前206－公
元8年）
直徑18.5厘米
館舊藏
銅鏡是古代照面飾容
的器具，通常爲圓
形。正面磨光，背面
有鏡鈕，並鑄刻着紋
飾及吉祥語句
Mirror with four-animal
patterns.
　Western Han Dynasty
(206 B.C.-8 A.D.)
D.18.5 cm.
Shaanxi History
Museum Collection.
The bronze mirrors
were used to reflect
face in ancient times,
generally round, with
front surface polish
-ed smooth and the
back cast with
designs and auspi-
cious languages.

四神規矩鏡
　　新莽（9－23年）
　　直徑19厘米
　　1956年陝西華陰出土
Mirror with four-lucky-
animal and T-L patterns.
　　Xin Mang period (9-23
　　A.D.)
　　D.19 cm.
　　Unearthed in 1956
　　at Huayin County,
　　Shaanxi.

尚方規矩鏡
　　西漢（公元前206－公
　　元8年）
　　直徑16.3厘米
　　1952年陝西西安出土
Mirror with T-L patterns.
　　Western Han Dynasty
　　(206 B.C.-8 A.D.)
　　D.16.3 cm.
　　Unearthed in 1952 at
　　Xi'an, Shaanxi.

四鸞銜綬紋平脫鏡
　唐（618－907年）
　直徑22.7厘米
　陝西西安出土
Mirror with the pattern
of four birds.
　Tang Dynasty
　(618-907 A.D.)
　D.22.7 cm.
　Unearthed from
　Xi'an , Shaanxi.

"仁壽"四神紋鏡
　　隋（518－618年）
　　直徑20厘米
　　1977年陝西西安出土
Mirror with the characters
of "仁壽" (Ren Shou) and
four-lucky-animal design.
　　Sui Dynasty
　　(581-618 A.D.)
　　D.20 cm.
　　Unearthed in 1977 at
　　Xi'an, Shaanxi.

十二生肖鏡
　　隋（581－618年）
　　直徑16.5厘米
　　館舊藏
Mirror with the twelve
animals (birth-year
symbols) design.
　　Sui Dynasty (581-618
　　A.D.)
　　D.16.5 cm.
　　Shaanxi History
　　Museum Collection.

雙獅鸞鳳紋八曲葵花鏡
　　唐（618－907年）
　　直徑21.5厘米
　　1951年陝西西安出土
Petal-shaped mirror with
double-lion and double-
phoenix pattern.
　　Tang Dynasty (618-907
A.D.)
　　D.21.5 cm.
　　Unearthed in 1951 at
Xi'an, Shaanxi.

雙鸞飛仙紋八曲葵花鏡
　　唐（618－907）
　　直徑14.3厘米
　　1973年陝西戶縣出土
Petal-shaped mirror with
double-phoenix and
flying Apsaras.
　　Tang Dynasty (618-907
A.D.)
　　D.14.3 cm.
　　Unearthed in 1973 at
Huxian County,
Shaanxi.

瑞獸葡萄鏡
　　唐（618－907年）
　　直徑18.7厘米
　　館舊藏
Mirror with lucky-animal
and grape patterns.
　　Tang Dynasty (618-907
　　A.D.)
　　D.18.7 cm.
　　Shaanxi History
　　Museum Collection.

鳥獸山水紋鏡
　　唐（618－907年）
　　直徑20.2厘米
　　1978年陝西乾縣出土
Mirror with birds, animals, hills and waters.
　　Tang Dynasty (618-907 A.D.)
　　D.20.2 cm.
　　Unearthed in 1978 at Qianxian County, Shaanxi.

龜紐八卦鏡
　　唐（618－907年）
　　直徑16厘米
　　1971年陝西西安出土
Mirror with "the Eight Diagrams" patterns and tortoise knob.
　　Tang Dynasty (618-907 A.D.)
　　D.16 cm.
　　Unearthed in 1971 at Xi'an, Shaanxi.

責任編輯　田小琳　葉岐生
Editor in Charge Tin Siu Lam　Ye Qisheng
撰　　文　李西興
Brief Introduction by Li Xixing
圖版說明　李西興　文　軍
Treasures Selected and Captions by Li Xixing Wen Jun
設計　屈利軍　陳嘉田
Designed by Qu Lijun Chan Ka Tin
英譯　穆善培　文　軍　白麗莎
English Translation by Mu Shanpei Wen Jun Bai Lisha
攝影　劉合心　邱子渝　華新民等
Photoes by Liu Hexin Qiu Ziyu Hua Xinmin etc.

陝西歷史博物館

《陝西歷史博物館》編寫組編

主編　尹盛平

副主編　李西興

陝西人民美術出版社
　　　　　　　　　　　　出版發行
香港文化敎育出版社

陝西人民美術出版社

地址：西安市北大街131號

電話：(029) 7211086

香港文化敎育出版社

地址：香港北角蜆殼街9-23號秀明中心24樓B室

電話：(00852) 2887 1120　傳眞：(00852) 2503 2580

大16開本　10印張

中文30千字　英文50千字

1994年9月第一版　1994年9月第一次印刷

書號：ISBN 7－5368－0499－7/J・429

~~印數：~~000冊

￥150.00